SO [illegible] WANNA BE A STUNTMAN

The Official Stuntman's Guidebook

Go for it!
Mark

Mark Aisbett

Aisbett, Mark, 1964 -
So you wanna be a stuntman : the official stuntman's guidebook

ISBN 0-9684865-0-9

I. Stunt performers — Vocational guidance. 1. Title.
II. Title: Official stuntman's guidebook.

PN1995.9.S7A48 1999 791.43'028 C99-900206-6

Published by Lifedrivers Inc.
P.O. Box 3772, Garibaldi Highlands, B.C., V0N 1T0

Produced and designed by Ad-dictive Productions,
Squamish, B.C., January 1999

Cover Photograph: Robert Kwong
Mark Aisbett doing a helicopter/train transfer for
Crackerjack II

Cover Design: Patricia Heintzman

First edition published 1999.

DISCLAIMER

This book is sold, or otherwise provided, on the understanding that the authors – Lifedrivers Inc. and Mark Aisbett – as the case may be, are not responsible for any result or results of any action or actions taken in reliance upon any information contained therein or presented thereat or omissions in relation thereto. It is further understood that the said authors, as the case may be, do not, pursuant to this book, purport to render legal, physical or other professional advice. The said authors, as the case may be, hereby disclaims all and any liability to any person, whether a purchaser of this book, or otherwise, arising in respect of this book, and of the consequences of anything done or purported to be done by any such person in reliance, whether whole or partial, upon the whole or any part of the contents of this book. If legal, physical or other professional advice or assistance is required, the services of a competent professional person should be sought. We recognize that some words, model names and designations, for example, mentioned herein are the property of the trademark holder. We use them for identification purposes only. This is not an official publication.

To all of the inspirational friends and family who have made this book possible: Monique Aisbett, Patricia Heintzman, Steve and Teresa Jensen, Gwen and Mike Young, Alan Jacques, Raymond Aaron, Lois Aisbett, Nancy Gaunt, Harv Eker, Marc Akerstream, Bill Wolfe and Ron Enns. And a sincere thanks to members of the stunt community who have supported and assisted in the fine tuning of this guidebook: Alex Taylor, Jacob Rupp, Kevin Andrushak, Kathy Hubble and Brian Rogne.

CONTENTS . . .

Chapter 1
Welcome 1

Chapter 2
History of Opportunity. 5

Chapter 3
Training 9

Chapter 4
Acting 19

Chapter 5
Padding and Equipment 25

Chapter 6
Resumé. 31

Chapter 7
Getting Work 37

Chapter 8
Set Etiquette 41

Chapter 9
A Day on Set 45

Chapter 10
Mental Preparation. 51

Chapter 11
Seven Steps to Ensure Success 57

Chapter 12
Professionalism. 63

Chapter 13
Money. 67

Chapter 14
Unions 71

Chapter 15
That's a Wrap 73

Appendices
i) Jargon 77
ii) Suggested Reading 82
iii) Contacts 83

1

WELCOME...

To the action-packed world of stunt performing

When I started out in 1987, I had many questions about the stunt business and the career choice I was about to make. Is stunt work for me? How do I go about getting my foot in the door? What kind of training do I need? Is there a demand for more stunt performers? Do I have the resolve and ability to do stunt work?

In 1987 there was nowhere to find answers. Today it's still extremely difficult to find these answers unless you know somebody who is a stunt performer and who is willing to help.

This guidebook was born from my desire for knowledge, and my frustration at the lack of information available. I've been working in this business for 11 years and my library of stunt-related literature totals five books. It is my sincere wish that I am able to help you along the path of what is, without doubt, the greatest, most exciting, ever-expanding business on earth.

Many people will tell you that it's not an easy road. Some people say the best advice to give someone who is thinking about getting into this business is to get out before you get in. The movie business is often characterized as glamorous and that is definitely a part of it. But it's a very small part of filmmaking and rarely has anything to do with the world of stunts.

This guidebook is designed to give you the information you need to start you on your way into the business of performing stunts. You will learn:

- How the business works
- Information on the unions and how to get in
- Specific training and how to train
- Training techniques for mind and body to help you perform to the best of your ability
- How to put together a resumé
- Where to find deals on padding
- And a whole lot more.

You have taken a very big step toward a career in the most exciting business on Earth. Although you haven't chosen the easiest job, it is one which can be incredibly rewarding.

Like all that is worthwhile in life, stunt work takes time and commitment. If you were to become a lawyer or surgeon you would expect to go to school for five to 10 years. Stunt work is no different. There is an infinite amount to learn and skills to refine in order to succeed. There is both an art and a science to performing a stunt safely and successfully. The good news is that most of what you will learn is fun, challenging and exciting, provided you are creative and like to be physical.

All the information you need to get started is here in these pages. The rest is up to you.

2 A HISTORY OF EXCITING OPPORTUNITY

"People say 'you're crazy Jackie!' Yes, I'm crazy, crazy about making movies."
– Jackie Chan

Opportunity is knocking on the door of the film industry even more than it was during the Hollywood boom days of the '50s. We are at the cusp of the greatest growth in North America's exciting movie business.

The film industry is growing by leaps and bounds. Since 1989 there has been incredible growth in both the number and quality of productions made and money spent in North America. The bottom line: the future is brighter than ever for those who choose a career in this industry.

The worldwide development of the video rental business is one reason behind this exponential growth in the film industry. In fact, the rise in film productions can be tracked directly to the increased popularity of video. The days of sitcoms and soaps have been eclipsed: instead of Happy Days re-runs, a quick trip to the local video store reveals a cornucopia of entertainment possibilities. There is also a trend back to the silver screen. Mega-theatres are sprouting up everywhere. Going to the movies is becoming an event again. Satellite receivers and expanding cable networks are also increasing the demand for more movies, more television shows and, thus, more commercials.

The integration of actors in computer and video games like Sega Genesis has also contributed to the increase of stunt opportunities. Combined with this growth is the fact that the popularity of action movies continues to rise: there is an ever-increasing proportion of movie budgets dedicated to stunts.

The film industry has never been so exciting. The time is *right* and the opportunity is *now* to pursue a career in stunts.

Read on!

3 TRAINING

The training trinity

My martial arts teacher, master Bill Wolfe, says that if you are going to train any physical skill there are three integral parts. At the bottom left corner of the training triangle is physical ability. You have to stay in good physical shape and be flexible enough to perform anything that is asked of you.

At the bottom right corner of the triangle are skills and techniques. Learn how to throw a sidekick or how to throw a punch for example. You have to train the actual techniques so that you continually improve and your skills ultimately become second nature.

Mental strength is at the pyramid's peak, and for good reason. You can get away without one of the bottom corners, but without mental tenacity you don't have a chance. You can workout constantly and have a black belt in a martial art, but if you lose your mental control in a fight, all of your skill is useless.

The three corners of the triangle work together holistically. There is no sense in only working on one or two. This holistic way of training when coupled with enjoyment accelerates how much and how quickly you learn.

Keep in mind that being adaptable is important when performing stunts. Take this into account when you plan your training. Think of skill diversity as insurance or money in the bank. And remember, you will never be asked to do something just the way you've practised it. There will always be something you have to do differently: your wardrobe will be in the way, you will have to emulate an actor's mannerisms, a vehicle won't work properly…or something.

I was on set one day and I had to climb a ladder for an actor. They got me to do the climb because it was high and overhanging at the top. When performing a stunt, you usually have to copy the actor's actions, but in this case I climbed first, so the actor had to copy my actions. I had observed him before so that I could emulate his general mannerisms, but the way I climbed the ladder was the way he had to climb it. He came over to be trained by me and my instructions went something like this:
"OK left foot up first, left hand up first, grab every second rung with your hands and use your feet on every single rung." He'd try and then I'd continue with: "OK, now stop, then take 3 steps and look up." We had been working on this for about 15 minutes when he looked down in exasperation and said, "It's never just climbing a ladder is it?!!?"

This incident has stayed with me. It's a good example of how nothing is simple or predictable in the stunt business. You are never asked to *just* climb a ladder or to *just* drive a car or to *just* throw a sidekick. There is always a curve thrown in. You are paid for your ability to deal with whatever gets thrown at you.

The Basics

Firstly, you should be physically fit. If you aren't fit, get in shape as quickly as possible. You are likely into some kind of sport or you wouldn't have picked up this guidebook. Whatever sports you are doing, and are good at, I suggest that you keep participating in them to keep yourself in shape and stay honed, especially if it's a skill that can be used in stunt work.

There are two skills that are critical in stunts: gymnastics and martial arts.

Gymnastics

Gymnastics teaches you many useful skills for stunts. Specifically, it teaches you air sense, a critical skill in stunt work. This is the ability to know where you are in the air in relation to the ground when you are upside down. Gymnastics also improves your flexibility, agility and develops strength.

There are gymnastics clubs in every city. Look in the Yellow Pages to find one in your area. The best clubs are the ones where other stunt performers train and these are the clubs you really want to find. They will teach you the specifics of gymnastics that pertain to stunts, and you will be able to talk to other stunt people about the film industry.

If you can't locate one of these clubs near you, join a local club but don't train the whole gymnastics curriculum. The disciplines you need to train for stunts are trampoline, mini tramp, and the floor exercises. The rings, uneven and parallel bars, balance beam and pommel horse are unnecessary in the beginning. The benefit of training gymnastics will become even more apparent later when you learn to use some of the more specialized stunt equipment like the air ram* and air ratchet*. (*See Jargon, Appendix i)

Martial Arts

The martial arts provide another very important set of skills to learn and train. There is a multitude of martial arts from which to choose. If you've never studied a martial art check out the many martial arts disciplines and the different schools. Meet the instructors to discuss their martial arts philosophy and determine their teaching style. You need to find one that fits both your personality and your schedule.

There are specific qualities to look for in a martial art which lend well to the stunt business. The flashy or more demonstrative martial arts are more appropriate for stunt work than the street-survival type of schools. The martial arts that emphasize high, jumping, spinning kicks and punches are more adaptable to stunt work. Big, spinning kicks look great on film which is the opposite of what works in real life.

Use this as a guide when you research schools. Look for an art that teaches punching, kicking and how to fall. It should also incorporate some kind of mental training such as breathing techniques, focus and concentration.

All of this doesn't mean much if you don't enjoy it. It has to *fit* you.

Skills you learn in martial arts which translate to stunt work are balance, timing, co-ordination, taking direction, focus, discipline, flexibility and, most importantly, the ability to calm one's mind. If you are already studying a martial art, keep it up, and concentrate on learning the flashy stuff. If you aren't, I suggest taking a look at Karate, Tae Kwon Do, Wu Shu, Kung Fu, Hapkido, Judo and Ju Jitsu. Choose one that best suits you.

Stage Fighting

Stage fighting is acting with a physical twist. It is the art of making something look painful that isn't and of making a staged fight look real. It has as much to do with camera angles as it has to do with the stunt people acting the fight. The camera has to be in the right location or the illusion is ruined and the audience will see that it wasn't a real hit.

Stage fighting is the opposite of real fighting. In stage fighting you rarely make contact. It's usually the person who gets hit that *sells* the hit and makes it believable. In a real fight you obviously don't want the other person to know that you are going to hit them. In stage fighting, you show them everything you are going to do *well* before you do it. In real fighting, you want to move as quickly as possible, but in stage fighting you have to slow everything down. Fake blood is used in stage fighting. In real fighting…well you get the picture.

Many of the techniques you learn in martial arts are not applicable when stage fighting. The skills you do keep are timing, concentration, focus and balance. Stage fighting can't be taught in a book. Find an experienced stage fighter and learn from him or her.

Always use a loose fist when practising stage fighting so that if you ever accidentally hit someone, you won't hurt him or her as much. This is important to remember when you punch a person in the stomach. You actually make contact with a stomach punch but because your fist is loose it isn't painful.

If you'd like to practise stage fighting on your own I suggest you watch movies, study the different reactions and hits, and try to simulate them. Watch the actions in slow motion and pay attention to the different camera angles that have been used to film a scene. Pay special attention to the timing of the hits, reactions and the flow of the fight. One of the best performers to watch is Jackie Chan, a consummate master at the art of stage fighting.

Stage fighting is the bread and butter of the stunt industry. It's an action which happens all the time in film scripts, and it's how many people get their start. An actor is scripted to take a punch or a kick and you look like them so you get called in for the day. Concentrate on practising and learning stage fighting, especially in the beginning. It's a learned skill which won't develop overnight. It takes time and training. Train and train and train and you'll be ready for the first job.

Climbing

Climbing is a unique skill to have. It helps with the peak of the training trinity: mental strength. It teaches you how to think clearly and perform safely in the face of fear. Physically, it offers enhanced flexibility, strength and balance. Many people who have the unique knowledge and skills which come with a climbing background work in the safety and rigging side of the film industry. From climbing you acquire diverse and important skills like rope handling, setting up and checking safe anchor systems, rappelling and, of course, climbing.

Weapons

You will need to learn how to handle and use firearms, so find a good gun-handling course. Check the industry magazines; sometimes gun handling courses are offered specifically for the film industry.

Other Skills

There are other disciplines that you can branch out into once you've developed these five skills. They include learning to drive a car quickly and precisely, learning how to spin a car and how to set up a car for spinning, horseback riding, motorcycle riding and especially motocross. The list goes on.

Summary

Train on a regular basis. Some of the skills you will be learning may be uncomfortable at first because they are new to you. It will take time and mistakes to perfect. You may be training with people who are experienced and this may make you feel self-conscious when you are first learning. But don't worry, persevere. Everyone has been there. Try to enjoy the process.

Don't train at 100 per cent. You don't make money when you are injured so always keep something in reserve so you don't hurt yourself. The time to really *go for it* is when you are getting paid and all the precautions have been taken.

When I first started out I trained with a person who always said, "Everyday I train is like money in the bank. For every three days of training I do right now I'm going to get one day of work someday." That person kept training regularly and consistently, and is now a stunt coordinator. It may seem like it takes a long time to get the money out of this *bank*, but with the right mind set, it's only a matter of time.

Kevin Andrushak getting "gelled up" for an explosion. "Stunt gel" as it is called, is used to protect bare skin when it will be exposed to fire.

4 ACTING

"In the end, everything is a gag."
– Charlie Chaplin

Acting is the foundation of the movie business so take acting classes. Good schools can be found in most metropolitan areas. The performers' union office is one source which can help you find a good school. It usually has up-to-date information on currently offered classes and can give you enough information so that you can make an educated choice. Acting will provide you with additional work opportunities. Going about getting acting jobs is different from the way you go about getting stunt work. Acting jobs require an agent, while stunt jobs don't.

Sign up with an agency

Stunt performers don't use agents to get stunt work. Agents will assist you in getting acting jobs but will rarely find you stunt work. When signing a contract with an agency, make it clear that it does not collect a commission on any stunt work that you find yourself.

Actors must have an agent. Actors who attempt to work

without an agency usually have very little hope of making a living in this business. Most productions deal exclusively with agencies. They rarely hire freelance actors because it is usually more trouble than it is worth. Agencies and production companies want to know exactly what they're getting. When dealing with an agency, a production company knows the standards for billing and payment. If a production books a freelance actor and he or she fails to show up for a job, the production is in trouble. When a production company works with an agency, however, it has some protection because the agency can send another person or track down the errant one.

It's also difficult to get top dollar when you represent yourself, whereas a good agent is an expert in this field. You may resent paying an agency a commission, but once you start making money, you'll appreciate the fact that your contracts, bills and deal-making are being handled by people who are more knowledgeable in this field than you.

The agency name on your acting resumé will open many doors and give you automatic credibility. An agent can also offer insurance for a performer in this business so that promises made are kept.

A two-way responsibility

Your agent is your liaison with the business world. Performers and agents must both make money from their association. As a result of this co-dependency, there exists a need and desire to help one another.

Agents will attempt to find clients for you and set up interviews and jobs. They will help you with your hair, makeup, and make important suggestions about your portfolio. They will collect your fees and make sure you are paid. An agent will also assist you in making the necessary contacts to enable you to work in another city or country.

Your responsibility

It's absolutely essential that you live up to your part of the agreement which includes keeping your agent informed of your whereabouts at all times. Having an answering service and a pager, and checking in with it regularly is helpful. Be a professional. Show up on time and ready to work. Your attitude must reflect your dedication.

Business is business

If you're not making money, if you have disciplinary problems or you let your appearance go, your agent may ask you to leave. If this happens, don't immediately blame the agency. Ask yourself a few introspective questions and answer them honestly. When an agent drops a performer, the reason is usually obvious.

It may also be necessary for you to switch agents. If you feel you're putting forth 100 per cent effort and yet you're not progressing in your career, perhaps you need a new agent. Make certain, however, that you've weighed the decision carefully. You may never be able to return to an agent you've previously left.

Steps to take in preparation for an acting audition

1. Make sure your agent has given you the time and address of the audition.

2. Know what part you are auditioning for.

3. Dress for the part.

4. Punctuality is a must. Allow yourself plenty of time for traffic delays.

5. Bring a bottle of water or juice. Waiting rooms can be hot and dry.

6. When you arrive, check your name with the receptionist and request a script if there is one.

7. Read the script and understand what it means.

8. Check the left side of the script to be sure you understand the mood and action of the film, TV show or commercial.

9. Find the essential *root* meaning of each sentence.

10. If your audition is for a commercial, discover the points the copywriter is trying to make. What market is he trying to hit? What sales problems does he face? If you understand these sales points, you are sure to please at least one member of the audition team — the writer.

11. Mark your script into sections, thereby finding major transitions (punch, transition, up and down voice inflection, coloring, pauses).

12. When you start to read, look the camera or auditioner in the eye and read the first line (at least) with your eyes off the page.

13. If you do not get the job, do not take it personally. For all you know the client insisted on using his nephew.

14. Go to your audition with a smile and leave with a smile.

After the audition

- Write your agent's name down on the contract if you received the job/commercial through an agency.
- Do not discuss money. Ask the production company to contact your agent.
- Beware of clients or producers who offer to take you around the world with them. Check with your agent for your own safety.

Acting and its relationship to stunts

Stunts are basically physical acting. There are times when you will be asked to act as part of your stunt. I strongly recommend that you take acting classes to assist you in making your stunts more believable.

5 PADDING AND EQUIPMENT

"If you want a guarantee, buy a toaster."
– Clint Eastwood

Padding is a personal thing. Every stunt performer has his *favorite* pads and his own way of *padding up* for a stunt. You will find that you are constantly on the lookout for better, smaller pads or a different way of protecting some part of your body. You will be bringing your pads with you whenever you are on set so you will need a bag that holds everything but isn't overly big.

Size is the main thing to look for when buying pads. Stunt performers are obsessed with finding small pads. Because all padding is hidden under clothes, the pads have to be as small as possible. If you have bigger pads you will find you can't often use them because they can be seen. Children's pads work well for just this reason. They are small but still substantial enough to protect you, provided they don't cut off your circulation.

The elastic on children's padding won't always go around your limbs. In this case, you can lengthen the elastic as needed: a seamstress can easily modify your pads to fit your body. Look for padding in sports stores, motorcycle shops, mountain bike stores and second-hand sports stores. Second-hand sports stores are a good place to find good, barely used children's pads at a much better price than buying new ones. If you do buy second-hand padding, get ones that aren't too old. The foam breaks down with time so the older they are, the less protection you will have.

You will also need bigger pads for the times you need the extra protection, have loose fitting clothing or need to make yourself look bigger because the person you are doubling is larger than you. Larger pads are easy to find. Look for the smallest padding you can get with the maximum protection. There are several great pads on the market due to the rising popularity of extreme sports. The mountain biking industry has developed some exceptional padding. Motocross, ringette and roller blading have good, adaptable padding as well.

Some basic pads you will need to get started

Back pad

This one is expensive, but also one of the most important. In my opinion, Dainese back pads are the best for stunt work. They protect well and don't protrude under clothing. You can usually find them in motorcycle stores. If you can't find one in any store you will have to order one. They come in different sizes so make sure you get one that fits properly.

Hip pads

Hockey Cooperalls are the standard hip protection in the industry because they are versatile: you can take out the pads you don't need. Ringette Cooperalls are also worth checking out because they are a little thinner compared to the ones designed for hockey. Get the smallest ones possible but keep in mind you will have to wear them for 14 or 16 hours at a time so they must be comfortable enough to wear for extended periods. Check out a great new hard-shelled hip pad made by a mountain biking company called V-Top.

Elbow pads

You will need at least two sets of elbow pads to get started. One set should be small and soft, and the other should be larger with a hard plastic shell. Children's small CCM Comp elbow pads are a good set because they offer good protection and are really small. Take out the inside cup and lengthen the elastic. These are probably the pads I use most often. You will also need a bigger set of elbow pads for the times you need the extra protection that the hard shell provides.

Knee pads

Have a soft and hard-shelled set of knee pads. There are some good slim high-density foam pads out there. Sports that have developed good knee pads are roller blading, skateboarding and volleyball.

Shin pads

Get a hard-shelled set of shin pads that covers your ankles as well as your shins. There are some really tiny hard-shelled junior shin pads that are suitable for all sorts of things. You can use them for the backs of ankles, forearms and biceps.

Kidney belt

Kidney belts help support your lower back. They are also useful in holding in the edges of pads that are sticking out and can be seen under your wardrobe.

Shoulder pads

Shoulder pads must be small. The second-hand sports stores are a good source to find these. You can usually get a pair of children's pads that fit well. You won't wear them much but when you can, they are nice to have on. You can also use them to make yourself look bigger if necessary.

Rib protection

Lacrosse equipment offers good rib protection because it is hard shelled.

Other things to include in your equipment bag:

- Sports tape for securing pads or taping an ankle.

- Duct tape — A million different uses.

- A towel to clean yourself or your pads up after a stunt.

- Mouth guard pre-fit to your mouth.

- Jock strap.

- Some small pieces of foam or flat kneepads are useful to fill in the gaps.

- A sports insole — Sorbathane ultra-sole, shock absorbing — makes it more bearable for when you are given dress shoes or combat boots that you have to run or jump in.

Once you get on set, talk to the other stunt people about the pads they use. Everybody has different items in their bag and you'll discover the latest and greatest.

Pads are a luxury in stunt work. The person you are doubling for and the clothes they wear will dictate what pads, if any, you can use. Men have it easier than women because their wardrobe usually covers more skin and they are meant to look bigger. Women in film must often wear tight-fitting or skimpy clothing.

One time when we were doing a lot of stair falls. We were all elegantly dressed: the men were in tuxes and the women were in evening dresses. The men could put on as many pads as they wanted under their tuxes, but the women couldn't get away with wearing any pads. Pads are a luxury for men much more often than women in this business.

Another time on set, I was wondering whether I should use the bigger pads or the smaller pads. Another stunt guy asked me if I could get away with the bigger pads under my wardrobe and I said I could. He said "Man, then use them!

Pad up so you can sell out." To sell out simply means to go for it. The more padding you have on, the higher you can fly and the harder you can land. So if your wardrobe is big or baggy and you can use the bigger pads, then use them.

6 RESUMÉ

Your ticket to ride

A resumé is what you give to the people who are going to hire you. It is something they will keep and will be their reference to you: what you can do, how good you are at doing it, what you look like and what you've done. Your talents, and how you list them, are extremely important. You want to shine the best possible light on your talents and skills without exaggerating them. This brings up an important point. Rule number one in this business is: never say you can do something you are not confident you can do. Describe your skills to the best of your ability and go with that. If you are worried that it doesn't look like you've done very much, don't worry, nobody's resumé is packed at first. Once you start training and working more, your resumé will start to take shape and look better.

When you first decide to become a stunt performer you need to understand that it is a major undertaking. There are so many things to learn. Understand and appreciate the fact that a successful stunt career does not happen overnight. It takes time so be patient. The beginning will be difficult because you are putting in a huge amount of effort with apparently few rewards.

The very first thing you need to do is to assemble your resumé. A stunt resumé is totally different from any other type of resumé. The first page consists of a head shot — a picture of yourself from the chest up. Get your name put across the bottom of the picture. It costs a little more but is essential. Remember, this is the image that will help get you work. The union office or industry magazines should be able to help you find a good photographer.

The second page of a stunt resumé lists a performer's specific stunt skills and film credits. Stunt skills are a large part of a resumé and should be listed as headings: martial arts, snowboarding, motorcycle, snowmobile, rock climbing, equestrian, surfing, driving, scuba diving, aviation (helicopter, planes), jet ski, in-line skating, gymnastics, weapons training, mountain biking.

Any skill that could be used in a stunt is a stunt skill. List your strongest skills first, then list the rest in descending order of expertise/experience. Include any previous experience in front of the camera and film credits, and list them from the most recent to the oldest. A stunt coordinator wants to see the name of the show, who the coordinator was and what you did. You may decide to list things under these headings:

Name of show *Coordinator* *Action*

Your height, weight, shirt size (neck and arm length), pants (inseam and waist), jacket, hat size, shoe size, hair and eye color, as well as your home telephone, cell phone, and pager numbers should be listed on the bottom of the page. You must have both a pager and a cell phone to be in this business. When you get a page from a stunt coordinator, they will often call two or three people at the same time and it's the first one to call back that gets the job. You need to be able to return a call as quickly as possible.

I was working at a construction job and a stunt coordinator called me. Since I only had a pager at the time, I ran off to find a phone which turned out to be 10 minutes away. I called him and he said that he wanted to hire me and he'd call me back in the afternoon to let me know the details. That afternoon the pager buzzed again and I ran to the phone. Ten minutes later I'm talking to the stunt coordinator. He asked "What took you so long?" I told him I was at work and there were no phones on site but that I got to a phone as soon as I could. He said that I was going to have to do something about the "lag time." I didn't think that 10 minutes was a big deal, but he did. I bought a cell phone the next day. I ended up working seven days for him on that show and made $15,000, which more than paid for the cell phone.

A resumé should be easily readable. Stunt coordinators get so many of them that all they want to do is glance at it and get all the information they need. They want to see what you look like, what you can do, and what you've done so far on film. Always be on the lookout for new ways to set up your resumé and new ways to improve it. Make it a reflection of your personality.

A resumé may look something like the following:

HIGH FALLIN' JONESY

Actra #555XYZ Sag #555ABC UBCP#555BCA

FILM & TELEVISION

Titanic	Mark Muldone	S.S.E.
Armageddon	Dave Yank	S.S.E.

STUNT SKILLS

Martial Arts
- Black belt in karate
- Total of 7 years training
- Currently training at Kingston Martial Arts Academy

Weapons
- Longstaff, tonfa, nunchakas
- Course on gun handling

Motorcycle
- Raced motocross for three years, 1992-1995
- Currently ride YZ 250 and GSX 750

Climbing
- 5.10 lead, multi-pitch
- Mountaineering
- Course on leading, rescue, 1998

Gymnastics
- Currently training at Somewhere Rec Center

Height: 6'1"	Shirt: 15.5/35	Shoes: 11.5
Weight: 163 lbs.	Pants: 32/34	Hair: Brown
Eyes: Blue	Jacket: 38 Tall	

Pager: (604) 555-3456 Cell/Message: (604) 555-7890

7 GETTING WORK

Experience and training are key

There are two things you have to concentrate on when you are starting out. One key element is training, which was discussed in Chapter 3. The other is to get on set. Getting on set and meeting the stunt coordinator is critical. Stunt coordinators are the people who hire you to do the job. They can't hire you unless they know you. Keep in mind that there is a fine line between being eager and being obnoxious. You have to let the stunt coordinators know who you are and what you're about, but not so much that you tick them off.

Once you have a resumé and a head shot, get the film list* (*see Jargon, Appendix i) for your area. It will list the addresses and phone numbers of production offices. Find out the names of the stunt coordinators and send them a copy of your resumé care of the production office. Include an introductory letter which states you are willing to help out so that you can learn more about stunt performing. Let them know you will follow up with a phone call, and make sure that you do. Send one of these packages, with a revised introductory letter, out once a month to television shows and to every new production office that opens.

The way to meet the different stunt coordinators is to get on set as an extra. Extra work gives you the required on set experience and is the way most people get into the business. No coordinator will hire you for a stunt if you don't know the basics of set etiquette and how a set operates. When you are an extra you are on set all day and much of your time is spent waiting for things like lighting and cameras to get set up. You have all day to find a minute to talk with the coordinator.

Once you meet a stunt coordinator, give them a resumé and let them know your background, what you're good at, and what you are training. Have questions ready for them and, if there is time, ask them about stunts. These are the people who have devoted their lives to this profession and know about the industry. They are your most valuable resource.

Once you've seen them for the first time don't expect your phone to start ringing off the hook. Remember, you're in a marathon, not a 100-metre sprint. Think of it as a numbers game: the more resumés you hand out and the more often you talk with a stunt coordinator, the more likely it is they will hire you. It's also a matter of experience. You need time in the beginning to build up enough experience on set so you know your way around, and know how things work. You also need this time to develop your skills so when you do get called for a stunt you can do a good job.

Gaining this experience takes years, but with perseverance you will become competent enough and know enough about the industry to be hired on a regular basis. It also takes years to get the training and time on set to enable you to do a good job consistently. I believe that if you persist and train, it will eventually happen.

8 SET ETIQUETTE

Play by the rules

1. Be sure you understand the exact nature of the job. If you do not know what you are supposed to do, ASK.

2. Bring everything you will need for the assignment with you. Don't expect to borrow.

3. Always go alone to assignments. Do not take friends, relatives or curious pals.

4. Learn the names of the people on set and use their names whenever possible.

5. Don't ask stupid or obvious questions. Listen and watch and most of them will be answered.

6. Don't litter in the dressing room (should you be lucky enough to have one). The studio or set is not your property so keep things tidy.

7. Treat wardrobe like gold. It is absolutely essential that all clothing and other items be returned in as good or better condition.

8. Be humble. Look at yourself as just another part of the crew. Learn to work with its members by being helpful and accommodating. Getting along with people is very important in this business.

9. On set everyone is *a good guy*. Never fault anyone on set.

10. Listen to the director or coordinator. A big part of this business is learning to take direction.

11. Do not constantly apologize. You can only depreciate your own value if you waste time apologizing for inexperience, clothes, hairstyle or appearance. You were likely hired because they thought you could do the job.

12. After you hear the word "rolling," it means that the cameras are rolling and they're filming a scene. DO NOT talk if you are anywhere near the set. The microphones used in film are very sensitive and can pick up small sounds a surprisingly long distance away.

13. Spend most of your time on set ready to work whenever possible. Make yourself available to help the coordinator in whatever way you can. This is also a great way to learn about the filmmaking process.

14. It is not productive to be insecure. Don't listen to that little voice inside your head that said you blew it. Think about the next line or movement.

15. Don't crucify yourself. Expect criticism and be grateful for it. It is not meant to criticize you personally, so use it constructively to improve.

16. Do not walk in front of the camera lens while a shot is being set up. Either walk around or duck under the front of the camera to avoid crossing the lens.

17. Do not stand in front of a light or bounce board* (*see Jargon, Appendix i). You may cast a shadow.

18. Never stand in an actor's line of sight.

19. Do not get in the way of the crew while they are setting up a shot. If you are new to a set, stay clear of the set up area.

20. Do not enter a studio when the red outer light is revolving. It means they are filming inside the studio. Wait until the light is off before entering.

21. While on location be very respectful of location owners, neighbors and business owners. Disrespect and bad manners are the cause of lost locations more than any amount of overshooting.

22. Take off all watches that beep at the hour and set all pagers and cell phones to mute or vibrate.

REMEMBER: Approach your assignment with a professional attitude. Time is the most valuable product your employers have to sell. Don't waste it.

9 A DAY ON SET

Why grow up when you can make movies

A day on set usually begins a day or a week before the stunt is to be performed with a call from the stunt coordinator. When you talk to the stunt coordinator, find out as much as you can about your task. As I explained earlier, the coordinator is very busy and doesn't have a lot of time to talk. Get your instructions, call time and location, whatever they may be, and write them down. If you have time before you go for the job, practise whatever it is that you are going to be performing. You can never be too prepared.

You should show up on set at least 30 minutes before your call time. Check in with an A.D.* (*see Jargon, Appendix i) as soon as you get there. He or she will show you to your dressing room and provide you with a contract which is important to fill out right away. Never go to set without a signed contract.

After you've completed all the paperwork, stop by the hair and makeup trailer and ask them when they would like to see you. They usually have a lot of people to get ready at the beginning of the day and they will be able to tell you when they can fit you in. If they want you right away, it's best to get at least the shirt on that you will be wearing on set so you won't be pulling wardrobe over your new hairdo and makeup.

If you have to put any pads on that you need to pull over your head, get them on as well. If you are going to be wearing pads on your upper body, put a T-shirt on underneath the pads to make it more comfortable. You may want a T-shirt over your pads as well to help hide the edges so that they don't show under your wardrobe. You can get a T-shirt to wear by asking nicely at the wardrobe trailer. If you have time, get into your wardrobe and be ready to go if hair or makeup needs you. If your wardrobe is not in your dressing room, you'll have to get it from the wardrobe trailer.

After hair and makeup, get into your full wardrobe including any pads you will need. It's not very comfortable sitting around in pads all day but that's just part of the job. Being ready means just that. When they are ready for you, don't make them wait while you get your pads on.

If the day is not too rushed, now is a good time to read the sides, the mini set of the lines and dialogue for the different shots that will be done that day. They also list the performers who are working that day and what scenes everyone will be working in. Read through the whole thing and go over the scenes that you will be in. Get a good idea of what's going on: the feelings and motivation of the characters you will be involved with. Start to visualize what you will be doing. The sides should be in your dressing room but if they're not, ask an A.D. and he or she will be able to find some for you. If you don't get a good enough idea about what's going on from the sides, find out from another source. Hair and makeup people are good to talk to, or speak directly with the coordinator.

Once you're ready to go, find the stunt coordinator and talk about the specifics of what you will be doing that day. If the stunt coordinator is on set, make sure to bring your gear bag with you, even if you will only be speaking together for a minute. Never go to set without your gear bag. This is an important rule. Often you'll get talking and an hour goes by and then they need you. Or because you're standing there they decide to use you for something that wasn't planned. Take your bag to set and stash it somewhere nearby but out of the way.

While on set, if you are doubling an actor, watch him or her study his or her mannerisms and the way he or she moves. Then practise what you have observed.

Performing the stunt on set

1. Listen for instructions. Add ideas after others have finished or when asked for them.

2. Don't jump the gun by saying, "It can't be done!" Work it out.

3. Always break the stunt into parts in your head. Visualize it and carry it out as planned.

4. If possible, try to have a look through the camera lens to see what will show and what you can get away with.

5. Stretch and warm up well in advance and away from the camera to avoid delays in production or the impression of showing off.

6. Any concerns should be discussed with the coordinator in private to avoid possible embarrassment to you and others.

7. Think of safety first. If you aren't ready, take the time to tell the coordinator.

8. Look for motivation from each scene, situation, wardrobe, lighting and surroundings.

9. Watch an actor's movements and actions so you can emulate his characteristics when doubling for him.

10. Slow down and relax. You always go faster than you think on film.

11. When performing as a stunt double, be conscious of the camera. Keep moving to avoid a proper fix on your face.

12. Don't get mechanical in your movements after several takes. Always perform the stunt like you are doing it for the first time.

13. Don't go to actors, directors, or producers to get praised for a stunt. If they like it, they'll tell you.

14. When complimented, accept graciously and give praise to the others involved in making it happen.

15. Try to catch daily rushes* (*see Jargon, Appendix i) as an aid in performance self-analysis.

Once you've been told that you're wrapped*, (*see Jargon, Appendix i) make your way to hair and makeup to take off any makeup and wash your hair if necessary. Go back to your dressing room, take off your pads and wardrobe, and get changed. No matter how late it is and no matter how tired you are, put your entire wardrobe back on its hangers and take it all back to the wardrobe trailer. However long you worked that day, the people in hair and makeup have been there longer, and they have to be there earlier than you do the next day. It's one of those small favors that means a lot.

Sign off with the A.D. Then go ask the stunt coordinator if there is anything else you can do before you leave. Pick up your pads or clean up something, doing whatever needs to be done. Say thanks for the day, so long, and we'll see you next time.

A "jerk off" (*see Jargon, Appendix i) performed for the TV series* Viper. *This stunt performer cracked open his helmet and was taken to hospital. It's not all fun and games.*

10 MENTAL PREPARATION

Playing the Head Game

"It's all in the mind," says Arnold Schwarznegger. "When I was young, I visualized myself being and having what it was I wanted. Mentally I never had any doubts about it. The mind is really so incredible. Before I won my first Mr. Universe, I walked around the tournament like I owned it. The title was already mine. I had won it so many times in my mind that there was no doubt I would win it. Then when I moved on to the movies, the same thing. I visualized myself being a successful actor and earning big money. I could feel and taste the success. I just knew it would all happen."

Your mental approach to stunt work will likely have the single greatest effect on your success.

What you do to prepare mentally before a stunt is individual. For some people, sitting alone, not talking to anyone is the trick to help them mentally prepare for a stunt. For others, that results in more nervousness. Some people prefer talking with others to take their mind off of the pressure of the next stunt. You have to experiment to find out for yourself what works and what doesn't.

Ayrton Senna — three-time Formula 1 driving champion — once said that the key to his driving aptitude and consistency was due to his ability to breathe effectively. Performing well, especially in stunts, can become easier and more consistent with a little knowledge about how to optimize your breathing. However, it is beyond the scope of this book to teach effective breathing. I suggest you take a course or find a teacher who can show you how to use your breathing to help maximize your performance. Being able to calm the mind and remain focused is an important skill to develop for stunt performing.

Being mentally prepared is a combination of things. There are certain techniques that can be used to help you get into the right mental state to perform well. The first is to train as much as possible. If you are confident in your skills you won't have as much negative mental chatter going on.

Learn to be aware of what your thoughts are in different situations. Pay particular attention to how your thoughts about yourself change in those situations. When you start in the stunt business it is normal to feel nervous and anxious. What do your thoughts tell you about yourself in these situations? Stand back and look at yourself objectively.

Instead of saying to yourself something like: "I'm going to screw this up" or "I haven't practised this enough" or "The camera is too close," you must exchange that thought for something more positive like, "This is going to be fun! Look where I am right now. Right where I want to be. Isn't this cool I get to go out, get shot and fall off that balcony. I love getting airtime!" The former *inhibits* the ability to think and perform and the latter *enhances* it. It's important to understand that they are only words we say to ourselves. The trick is knowing what we are saying and being able to change it to something that enhances what we are doing. A stunt coordinator once said to me, "If I need somebody to jump off a balcony, I'm going to go looking for a guy who just loves to jump!"

> "
>
> *When you first start a stunt, when you're waiting to go is actually the worst part of it. When they say roll the camera, and they say action, it now becomes work. You have to isolate everything else and totally focus on what it is you're doing. It takes 100 per cent concentration and there is no fear to it.*
>
> "
>
> *— Dar Robinson*

Visualization is using your imagination to see yourself succeed in a situation that hasn't yet happened. It is picturing yourself having or doing the thing you want, and successfully achieving the results you desire. Visualization is an important technique when performing stunts. Sometimes you don't get a chance to actually practise a stunt before doing it, so your ability to visualize it is extremely important. Many studies on visualization come to the same conclusion: visualization practice is almost as good as physical practice.

Visualization is a skill that can be trained like anything else. And the training is usually really fun. In your mind, picture yourself playing your favorite sport or performing a stunt correctly with energy. There are a few things to keep in mind when you are visualizing. Firstly, relax. The calmer the mind is, the better visualization works. Secondly, think only of success. The best thing about visualization is that you get to do it perfectly every time. Since you're practising, make sure you practise the right thing. Thirdly, make your visualization as detailed as possible. Enter the role and become it in your mind. See it, smell it, taste it, touch it, feel it.

When you are getting ready to do a stunt you will have many things to remember — your head should be tilted this way, your mouth has to be open, left hand in front, right hand behind, hit that mark, don't show your face. The conscious mind can only think of one thing at a time. Visualize your body doing the whole action properly. Visualize the stunt as a whole.

Once you've practised enough in your mind that you can see yourself doing the action properly, then choose a few key words that will trigger the action as it happens. If you have to run around a corner and get shot, your trigger words might be run-corner-stop-react-dead. The words you use are your own.

I was getting ratcheted (*see air Ratchet, Jargon, Appendix i) a long way one time and the director wanted to see a lot of flailing of my arms and legs. All I could think of was that I looked like a fish thrashing around on the end of a hook. So when it came time to do the stunt I screamed in my mind FISH! Your key words are whatever seems right for you at the moment.*

If you find yourself thinking counterproductive thoughts as you start a stunt, remember that you can only think one thought at a time. It is impossible to *stop* thinking about something; the only thing you can do is *replace* the unwanted thought with a thought that will help you to successfully accomplish the stunt. When you find yourself thinking incorrectly, replace the negative mind chatter with something that will help you to succeed.

One time we were filming a big scene with 70 or 80 stunt people and some extras. We all had to react at the same time. There was a countdown: 3, 2, 1, go! We all had to throw ourselves onto or over whatever it was that we happened to be standing beside. I was pulled from the back of the scene up to the front because there were less experienced people right in front of the cameras and the coordinator was worried about their timing. I was put beside a person who was just starting out, and we were both put right in front of the cameras. Just before we were ready to shoot I asked him if he was ready to go. He said: "Well I guess so, but we are right in front of the cameras and if we screw up everyone will see it. This is a lot of pressure." His mind was filled with counterproductive thoughts.

We all have counter productive thoughts from time to time. The trick is to be aware of them and be able to drive them out with constructive thoughts. Muhammad Ali would get into the ring and say over and over "I'm the greatest, I'm the greatest, I'm the greatest." What he was effectively doing was driving out any unwanted negative thoughts with a message that he knew would help produce the outcome he desired. So choose a mantra, a little chant that you can say over and over to yourself, that will drive out unwanted chatter.

Another thing to be aware of is your energy level. If your energy is too high, your performance may be erratic. If your energy is too low, your reactions may not be quick enough. There seems to be a mental zone that is optimal for performance. A good way to control your level of energy is through your breathing. If your energy is down, try a few quick, deep breaths through your mouth. If your energy is too high take slow deep breaths through your nose. Breathing through your nose has a calming effect while breathing through your mouth gets the blood flowing. What you want to be able to do is to enter a mental zone that will allow you to think quickly and calmly at the same time. It's different for everyone. The key is to be aware of *your* energy level and the level at which *you* perform best.

Bad hair days

11

SEVEN STEPS TO ENSURE SUCCESS

In stunt performing or anything else in life

1. Always be early

Don't *try* to be on time. If you are *trying* to get somewhere on time then you're already late. In stunts it is imperative that you are early. There are no excuses. Period. Whether you are working or not, cultivate a habit of always showing up early. When you have a day on set you should get there at least 30 minutes before your call time. That way if you get a speeding ticket on the way to work, or there is an accident or heavy traffic, you will still get there on time. Remember, no excuses.

2. Do what you say

Sounds easy but the truth is that most people have the irritating habit of committing themselves to something they either have little intention of doing or the ability to complete. Do you always do what you say you're going to do? If you're honest with yourself then the answer is probably no. Develop the unique ability to remain steadfast in your commitments. Know your limits. Again, make it a habit in your everyday life to watch what you say and remain honest enough with yourself to know when to say no or yes.

3. Always say "please" and "thank you"

Now you may groan and say, "give me a break," but the fundamental politeness of saying please and thank you are modicums of respect often forgotten. It's a small gesture that expresses respect and demonstrates a good attitude. It could be the difference between movie watching or being in the thick of the action.

4. Don't leave home without your resumé

Just like the boy scout motto says: "Be prepared." You just never know when you'll meet someone who will be able to further your career. A stunt coordinator may walk across a set on which you're an extra. You may be careening (practising in a responsible manner of course) down a city street and stumble upon film trucks and have an opportunity to hand out your resumé. Make it a habit to be prepared, resumé in hand.

5. Train

Make a habit of training what is uncomfortable. A lot of the skills you will need to become an accomplished stunt performer are not necessarily abilities you already possess. You need to keep training whatever you are good at and keep those skills honed, but you should also focus your training on what you are not good at. There is a whole range of skills needed to perform stunts as discussed in Chapter 3. You will naturally develop your specialties but career advancement will be found in your ability to adapt and in your versatility. It's only a matter of time before you become proficient at whatever it is you are training, if you do it consistently.

6. Get on set

Learn about filming by becoming a student of the film industry. Observe, see and take it all in. Stunt work is not an insular world. It is part of a greater whole, the film industry, with which it is integrally entwined. One of the most enigmatic aspects of the film industry is that you can never learn it all. So never believe that you have done so. Every time you get on set is a valuable learning experience. The key is to get on set whenever possible, whether it is as an extra or a special skills extra. When you get on set, look, listen and learn. Watch how the filming is done: become a lifelong student.

7. Use your ears more than your mouth

God gave us two ears and one mouth for a reason: to listen at least twice as much as we talk. Factor in the film biz "mouth shut, ears open" quotient and listen far more than you talk. The one sure-fire way to end your career prematurely is to talk too much. This business naturally seduces out-of-control egos. The overabundance of ripe egos in the industry is legendary and everybody is on the lookout for cocky blabbermouths. Being humble is always the best policy.

Summary

This business is built on relationships and trust. One of your main tasks is to build strong relationships with the people you work with. In the beginning, do as much as you can to develop this sense of trust and dependability. Concentrate on the small details that give initial impressions. Trust starts with little things like showing up on time, looking clean and being prepared. When you get a job, show up on set prepared, have all the padding that you will need, arrive full of energy and perform with energy.

Stunt coordinators have the responsibility of designing the stunts, preparing a budget for the action, and making sure filming gets done safely and within budget. To do this, they need to know that they can depend on the people they have working with them. Stunt coordinators look for people they can count on. They are looking for consistency and dependability more than raw talent.

12 PROFESSIONALISM

What is it?

True professionals give one the good feeling of being well looked after. They have the know-how to solve your problem, and if not, they aren't afraid to say they'll have to look into it and get back to you. You have the feeling that they really do care to give you the best possible service.

People may be professionals because of their attitude toward work, a pride in the work that they do and their sense of responsibility toward other human beings.

Professionalism is an attitude that should ideally be employed by all workers regardless of their specific occupations. Professionalism is associated with responsibility, dependability and a serious attitude toward one's job.

Professionalism is the process of approaching a job or situation seriously, paying particular attention to detail. Boring age-old worn-out qualities? Certainly not. They are qualities that get the job done, qualities that employers respect and qualities that get you noticed in a world where recognition means career advancements, landing jobs or signing contracts.

A professional is someone who is multi-faceted and who has developed a level of expertise. A professional is always open to new ideas and growth, and complements that by developing a lifestyle outside the working environment, thus creating a balance of the total person.

Another aspect of professionalism, which many people fail to recognize, is courtesy. How much does it cost to write a thank you note to someone who has been especially helpful to you? How often does it happen? This rarity alone should give you an indication of how much favorable interest you can attract to yourself through the simplest of means. A verbal thank you is always acceptable, but a written note becomes a permanent reminder of your appreciation.

Courtesy also means remembering to keep your promises. "I'll call you Tuesday" should mean just that. It is, after all, an aspect of follow through. Professionalism is follow through, and meeting your commitments on time: efficiently delivering the goods.

To be professional in whatever you do is to know the job you are doing thoroughly and do it to the best of your ability. You must keep up with the latest developments in every aspect of the type of work you are involved in and apply what relates to your particular job to keep you current and up to date. You must have integrity in every aspect of your work, in your dealings with co-workers, employers and clients alike.

Professionals pay attention to the element of preparedness. They are willing to do the extra research to familiarize themselves with a new project. They take the time and trouble to find out who to approach for information. Professionalism can be as simple as doing your homework so that you can feel at ease when you open your mouth.

To become a professional takes a melding of many qualities. Each person gives it his or her own individual touch. Perhaps it is best summed up by this: if you can go home at the end of the day and feel good about what you have done, then you are probably doing a professional job.

Kathy Hubble and Brian Rogne taking a dive for A Stranger In Town.

13

MONEY

A stunt performer is paid in a few different ways

Current union wages in Canada

- Daily rate — Approximately $500 for the first eight hours.
- Time and a half — eight to 11 hours.
- Double time — 11 hours and up.
- Adjustment — $100 and up based on a stunt's difficulty and danger.
- User Fees — A pre-payment of residuals the producer pays to be able to use your image on screen for a set amount of time, usually four or five years. Sometimes there are residual payments which come over time as a show airs instead of an up front pre-payment. These are rare in Canada but more common in the U.S.

Pre-payments — often known as buyouts — are a percentage of your daily rate, plus overtime, plus adjustment. Right now, on union shows, the buyouts range from 75-130 per cent depending on the type and amount of distribution. So if you were to take an eight-hour day, on a TV show at a $100 adjustment, and a 105 per cent buyout, your total for the day would look like this: (500+100)x105%=$1,230. A usual day is 10 to 14 hours. Sometimes you make a little less and sometimes you make a little more, but usually you take home between $1,000 and $2,000 per day.

Current union wages in the United States

- Daily rate — Approximately $600US for the first 8 hours.
- Time and a half — 8 to 10 hours.
- Double time — 10 hours and up.
- Adjustment — Whatever you negotiate.
- Residual Payment — It will be paid if you or your stunt is recognizable. This payment varies depending on how much money the show makes, how many stunt people worked on the show, how many times it airs and several other factors. If the show makes a lot of money, you make a lot of money. If it doesn't do too well, you don't make as much.

Keep in mind that these are union wages. When you first start out, your work might be non-union, which is completely different regarding wages. It's usually a one-time payment. No buy out, residual, or overtime. For these jobs you just negotiate the best deal you can, then decide if it's worth it. I would caution against this type of work for a number of reasons. Firstly, the safety standards are usually a lot lower than union shows so there is a greater chance of injury. Secondly, it will not advance your credibility with professional stunt coordinators. Thirdly, once you become an apprentice member, union rules preclude you from accepting such work.

At first glance these wages may seem like a lot of money but it's deceiving. When you are starting out, you are asked to do simple stunts. The money you earn is disproportionately high to the task you are performing. After you get established, you are asked to perform more difficult or dangerous stunts. This is when the risk becomes disproportionate to the money.

You just can't beat locations like this one. Filming a Jeep commercial in the Tantalus Range of the Coast Mountains, British Columbia.

14

UNIONS

Just another part of the game

The Alliance of Canadian Cinema, Television, and Radio Artists (ACTRA), is comprised of performers working in recorded media throughout Canada. The Union of British Columbia Performers is the autonomous branch of ACTRA in British Columbia. Both organizations negotiate standard collective agreements with large groups of Canadian and non-Canadian producers for application in their respective jurisdictions. Membership in one organization is membership in both.

You can qualify for membership in the union by earning six credits towards membership. In general terms, you earn a credit towards membership each time you are contracted to work in a residual attracting category on a production, for a period of up to one week. If you work on two different shows in the same week, that would mean two contracts and two credits. For every contract you work, you will pay a permit fee until you have full membership. It is important to remember to register with the union as an apprentice member within six weeks after receiving your first credit, otherwise you will lose the credit toward membership.

Becoming an apprentice member is beneficial in other ways as well. Apprentice members receive preference of engagement in all performing categories from producers over non-members. This means that producers must first consider you for work before considering any non-members who may be available. This can be particularly helpful when you are starting out. For example, when you decide to do extra work in order to gain valuable on-set experience, having preference of engagement as an apprentice member will allow you to work more often and at a higher rate of pay than would otherwise be the case. You will also be able to attend union meetings, and start receiving union newsletters that will keep you up to date on all of the productions shooting in your area. You should make a point of getting involved as much as you can with your union. Doing so will give you valuable insight into the business side of show business, and help you make contact with other performers who share your goals and aspirations.

The Screen Actors Guild (SAG) and the American Federation of Television and Radio Artists (AFTRA) are the two union bodies in the United States. SAG handles TV and film and AFTRA handles video productions.

There is no apprentice membership in SAG. To get into SAG you need either three days as an extra on a union voucher, or one day working in a principal category, or one year with a principal contact with AFTRA. You don't need any credits to join AFTRA.

Getting into the union is your first big hurdle.

15 THAT'S A WRAP

Persistence is more important than talent

There is a saying that there is nothing more common than talented people who are getting nowhere. Talent, skill and technique alone will not get you very far in this business. They are necessary but they are only the tools of the trade. Your tenacity and persistence mean so much more.

It should be obvious by now that there is not an easy road ahead. Stunt performing is a profession that takes commitment, skill, a positive attitude and, above all, adaptability. Especially at the beginning when jobs are few and far between.

You may get a call and have to tell your boss that you can't make it that day because you have a stunt to do. You may plan a weekend away and then have to cancel at the last minute because your pager goes off. These types of things are all part of being a stunt performer. Your adaptability will be tested in all kinds of ways, not just on set.

Take the information in this book and put it to good use. Start training and keep training. Cultivate positive habits.

Get on set and meet coordinators and other stunt performers.

Learn about how the industry works and how filming is done. Like anything in life, it all comes down to whether you want it badly enough or not. I believe that those of you who persist *will* make it.

I hope that this book helps you on your path to becoming the greatest stunt performer that you can be.

Good luck!

APPENDIX 1

Jargon

- ACTRA — Alliance of Canadian Cinema, Television, and Radio Artists.
- A.D. — Assistant Director. There are usually three or four A.D.s per show, sometimes more. Basically they act as a liaison between the director and the rest of the crew to make sure that everything runs smoothly. The 1st A.D. works full time with the director. The 2nd, 3rd and 4th usually work with the crew.
- Air ram — A catapult which uses a blast of compressed nitrogen to launch a stunt performer high into the air. Commonly used for explosions.
- Air ratchet — A big piston which uses a blast of compressed nitrogen to pull a stunt performer backwards at a high rate of speed. Commonly used for point blank gunshot blasts.
- Apple box — Plywood boxes used to elevate gear and sometime people on set. There are full, half and quarter apples.
- Background — Extras used to fill in the back of a scene. Extras will usually hear a call for "action" and then they will hear their cue, which is "background action."

- Beat — A slight pause in the action. "Give it a beat after action before you come in."

- Bounce board — A reflective board or screen that *bounces* the light back on the set so that light is not aimed directly at the set.

- Breakaway glass — What stunt people go through instead of real glass. It's actually real glass but specially tempered so it breaks into tiny pieces instead of big, pointy shards.

- Call time — The time that you have to show up a half-hour before. You will get your call time from the stunt coordinator.

- Cheat — Is when you move something in a scene. Sometimes it's for a camera angle; sometimes it's to give a little more room for a performer. "Cheat that desk over to the right a little."

- Circus — Is the group of honeywagons, trailers, catering trucks and tents you get when filming on location.

- Daily rushes (or dailies or rushes) — Raw footage from the previous day's filming shown to the director and key personnel to make sure that what they filmed is acceptable.

- D.O.P. — Director of Photography. Head honcho of the camera department.

- Extras holding — Is a place where extras hang out until they are needed.

- Fernie — Short for furniture pad or blanket. Used for all kinds of things.

- Film list — A list of all current productions being filmed in your area and obtainable at the union office.

- First positions — That's where you start your action from. After you've done a take and they want another one somebody will shout, "Back to first positions!" Whenever you do anything in front of the camera, always remember where you started from.

- Gaffer tape — Duct tape, 600-mile an hour tape.

- Gag — A stunt.

- Head Shot — A head and shoulders photograph of yourself to be given to stunt coordinators along with your resumé.

- Honeywagon — A trailer or group of trailers that have washrooms, dressing rooms and the A.D. office.

- Hot — The word hot usually means a gun or explosion. If you are going to be involved with either of these in a scene they won't load the gun or put power to the explosives until just before they are ready to go. When they do, that gun or explosive is *hot*.

- Hot set — A set that has already been used and needs to stay the exact same way because it might be re-used.

- IATSE — International Alliance of Theatrical and Stage Employees.

- Jerk off — A stunt using a combination of cables and ropes to "jerk" a stunt performer "off" a motorcycle. This is usually painful.

- M.O.W. — Movie of the week.

- N.D. — Non-descript. An N.D. stunt means you are not doubling for anybody.

- On the day — Means when the time comes to shoot. "On the day I want you standing over there by that street lamp ready to go."

- P.A. — Production Assistant – A person employed to generally help out with filming. They have numerous jobs from crowd control, to clean up, to public relations.

- Picture car — Is any car used in a scene.

- Picture is up — Means that the rehearsals are over and we're ready to shoot.

- Rolling — Means that the cameras are rolling and the director is just about to call action.

- Sell out — Go for it, give it your all, no holds barred. In other words, hit that ground hard.

- Set — Where the actual filming is being done.

- Squib — A small explosive charge rigged with a packet of fake blood that is put on your body. It is used to make it look like you've been shot. They can do some serious damage if you get an appendage in the way.

- S.S.E. — Special Skills Extra. An extra who performs an additional skill. Some examples are: riding a bike, skateboarding, or driving a car. They are sometimes used in the background of an action scene.

- Wrap — The end of the day. "That's a wrap, time to go home."

APPENDIX II

Suggested Reading

Mental Preparation

Thinking Body, Dancing Mind
by Chungliang Al Huang and Jerry Lynch

The Inner Athlete
by Dan Millman

Mind Power
by John Kehoe

The Art of Breathing
by Nancy Zi

Film

The Fall Guy: 30 years as the Duke's Double
by "Bad Chuck" Robertson with Bodie Thoene

Burns, Falls and Crashes
by David Jon Wiener

Stuntman, The Autobiography of Yakima Canutt
by Yakima Canutt and Oliver Drake

Stunt People
by George Sullivan and Tim Sullivan

Guide to Film Production Terms
by Tim Moshansky

Any biographies or autobiographies of people you admire.

APPENDIX III

Contacts

CANADA

ACTRA – The Alliance of Canadian Cinema,
Television and Radio Artists
Head office - 2239 Yonge Street.,
Toronto, Ontario M4S 2B5
Tel-416-489-1311, Fax-416-489-8076,
Toll Free-1-800-387-3516
www.actra.com

UBCP – Union of British Columbia Performers
200-856 Homer St., Vancouver, B.C. V6B 2W5
Tel-604-689-0727
Fax-604-689-1145

UNITED STATES

SAG – Screen Actors Guild
5757 Wilshire Blvd.
Los Angeles, California
90036
Tel-323-549-6768
Fax-323-549-6775
www.sag.com

AFTRA – American Federation of Television and Radio Artists
5757 Wilshire Blvd.
Los Angeles, California, 90036
Tel-323-634-8100, Fax-323-634-8246
www.aftra.com

ADD TO THE LIST

ABOUT THE AUTHOR

Mark Aisbett got into stunt performing in 1987. He was rock climbing in Squamish, British Columbia, when he met a guy who was a stunt performer and they started talking about driving. The discussion soon diverted to the film industry.

"If you ever need a guy to drive give me a call," was what Mark said to get his foot in the door.

Two months later he got a call and was asked to join a newly formed stunt group to learn the tricks of the trade. Shortly thereafter he got his first job in *Distant Thunder* starring Ralph Macchio and John Lithgow. He played an American GI heli-sidegunner in Vietnam. "I got to hang out of a helicopter for four days and I thought to myself, 'This is it, this is what I want to do for a living'."

Today, Mark is an active stuntman in B.C.'s booming film industry. His film and television credits include *Rumble in the Bronx, Mr. Magoo, Unforgettable, Outer Limits, Millennium, Viper and K2* to name just a few. Mark has also been a driving instructor at Westwood/Mission raceways since 1989. He is an experienced rock climber and race car driver. Mark and his wife Monique live in Brackendale, just north of Squamish, British Columbia.

SO YOU WANNA BE A STUNTMAN

The Official Stuntman's Guidebook

Would someone you know benefit from reading "The Official Stuntman's Guidebook"?
It has proved to be the ideal gift for sports-minded people, athletes and anyone with a love of thrills and adventure.

Please rush me ____ copies of The Official Stuntman's Guidebook, at $19.95 US each plus $4.99 US or
$25.95 Cdn and $5.99 Cdn shipping & handling.

I am enclosing a cheque/money order payable to Lifedrivers Inc. in the amount of $__________.

NAME AND ADDRESS IN BLOCK LETTERS
Name ______________________________
Address ______________________________
Postal/zip code __________ Province/state __________
Country ______________ Telephone __________
Fax ________________ E-mail ____________

We offer a discount on orders of 10 or more books.

Lifedrivers Inc.
Box 3772, Garibaldi Highlands,
B.C., Canada, V0N 1T0
www.actionstunts.com

Please allow three to four weeks for delivery.

FOR MORE INFORMATION

We welcome all stories, comments, questions and suggestions that you may have. For a free information package with the latest educational material on stunt performing, please contact us at:
Tel 1-888-622-6543, Fax 1-888-622-6544.

Lifedrivers Inc.
Box 3772
Garibaldi Highlands,
B.C, Canada, V0N 1T0
www.actionstunts.com